YOUR KNOWLEDGE HAS VALUE

Anderson Brians

Impact of Globalization on Hospitality

GRIN Verlag

Bibliografische Information der Deutschen Nationalbibliothek:

Die Deutsche Bibliothek verzeichnet diese Publikation in der Deutschen National-
bibliografie; detaillierte bibliografische Daten sind im Internet über http://dnb.d-
nb.de/ abrufbar.

Imprint:

Copyright © 2011 GRIN Verlag GmbH
Druck und Bindung: Books on Demand GmbH, Norderstedt Germany
ISBN: 978-3-656-40637-2

This book at GRIN:

http://www.grin.com/en/e-book/211918/impact-of-globalization-on-hospitality

GRIN - Your knowledge has value

Der GRIN Verlag publiziert seit 1998 wissenschaftliche Arbeiten von Studenten, Hochschullehrern und anderen Akademikern als eBook und gedrucktes Buch. Die Verlagswebsite www.grin.com ist die ideale Plattform zur Veröffentlichung von Hausarbeiten, Abschlussarbeiten, wissenschaftlichen Aufsätzen, Dissertationen und Fachbüchern.

Visit us on the internet:

http://www.grin.com/

http://www.facebook.com/grincom

http://www.twitter.com/grin_com

Introduction

The rapid development of international economic integration and globalization has led to significant changes in hospitality industry. Therefore, it is necessary to dwell on various aspects of globalization as the process influencing the current and future developments in hospitality industry. This research will be based on the assumption of a generally beneficial impact of globalization on the industry's development, and the analysis presented here will seek to substantiate this claim.

For the purposes of this discussion, globalization shall be defined as the "ever-tightening network of connections which cut across national boundaries, integrating communities in new space-time combinations" (Hall 1992, p.299). While this definition may seem excessively broad, it is likely to better encapsulate the essence of globalization than the explicitly economy-oriented ones.

This paper shall deal with the various expressions of globalization influences in modern hospitality industry. Given the extremely important role of the multinational corporations (MNCs) in contemporary tourism and hotel sectors, a case study of Hilton Hotels Corp. as the paragon of the globalized hotel chain will be integrated in this research. Further, a Business Performance Management (BPM) theoretical model shall be employed to evaluate the comparative performance of the prominent global hotel chains. Proceeding from the latter, a preliminary conclusion on the present state of the market may be formulated. Similarly, the problems of labour market and technological innovations shall be integrated into the study's research framework. Finally, the issue of business strategies shall be raised, with several examples thereof being subjected to comparative analysis.

The MNCs and the State of the Global Hospitality Market

Knowles, Diamantis, & El Mourhabi (2004) observe that the development of standardized hotel and restaurant chains may be one of the most prominent impacts of globalization on the modern hospitality industry. In particular, such regions as East Asia would appear to be particularly affected by the rise of the multinational hotel chains (Knowles, Diamantis, & El Mourhabi 2004, p.18), with British and U.S. hotel chains being especially prominent in this regard. Hence, in order to receive a more objective view of the global hospitality industry, one should review the phenomenon of the rise of the MNCs in hospitality market.

According to Cheng, Wang, & Chu (2011), the combined number of hotel room controlled by 9 largest hotel chains, or "nine giants" (2011, p.214), amounted to 2.98 million in 2009, as opposed to 2,84 million in 2005. In the percentage terms, the total market share of these companies would amount to more than 75%, making the world hospitality market increasingly monopolized (Das & De Groote 2008, p.4). Thus, the examination of these companies' business situation and their responses to the changes in market trends would enable the researcher to formulate more general perspectives on the state of the industry at large.

Das & De Groote (2008) present a comprehensive account of the situation of the world's top hotel chains. They observe that while in the 1980s, the U.S.-based were retaining their grasp over the market, from the 1990s onwards, the UK and even East Asian hotel chains have begun to advance to the external markets as well. Such hotel chains as Mandarin Oriental and Shangri-La Hotels have opened several hotels in Paris and other major European cities, hoping to attract additional customer base (Das & De Groote 2008, p.3). Nevertheless, the major players in the global hotel market still include predominantly Western corporations. Table 1 includes some data on the comparative business performance of 10 main multinational hotel chains, with the data provided as of October 2007. The table, reproduced below, is found in Das & De Groote (2008, p.5).

Rank in 2007	Group	Rooms 1995	Hotels 1995	Rooms 2007	Hotels 2007	Evolution, 1995-2007
1	InterContinental (UK)	356,800	1,925	556,246	3,741	56%
2	Wyndham Worldwide (USA)	413,891	4,208	543,237	6,473	31%
3	Marriott (USA)	184,995	874	502,089	2,775	171%
4	Hilton Corporation (USA)	*147,457	388	497,738	2,901	238%
5	Accor (France)	256,607	2,265	486,512	4,121	90%
6	Choice (USA)	293,796	3,358	429,401	5,316	46%
7	Best Western (USA)	280,144	3,409	315,401	4,164	13%
8	Starwood (USA)	132,477	425	265,598	871	100%
9	Carlson (USA)	79,482	349	145,933	890	84%
10	Global Hyatt (USA)	77,512	167	141,011	733	82%

Source: Das & De Groote 2008. Please note that the 1995 data for Hilton Corporation are the sum of indices for Hilton International and Hilton Corporation, as these ventures were integrated only in December 1995.

As one may discern from the data presented above, the period between 1995 and 2007 saw the especially explosive development of the multinational hotel chains, with further structural inequalities emerging among these latter. In particular, some hotel chains, e.g. Hilton Corp. or Marriott, appeared to benefit the most from the globalization of hospitality market, doubling or even quadrupling their number of hotels and hotel rooms controlled, while some other operators, such as Best Western or Wyndham Worldwide, either stagnated or grew at the lower rate than their competitors. Nevertheless, a clear picture of the general growth in the MNCs' presence in hotel market is tangible here, indicating the positive impact of globalization processes on their operating capacities.

However, it is still necessary to analyze the factors having an impact on the companies' comparative performance in the global market. To this end, a case study of Hilton Corp. has been conducted by the researcher, with a view to analyzing the possible business management factors that allowed this company to achieve such an impressive performance in the worldwide hospitality market. For this purpose, the BPM integrative model has been used to focus on Hilton Corp.'s strategic management proficiencies.

The Hilton Corp. as the Global Hotel Operator: A Case Study

The recent growth in Hilton Corp.'s market share has led to the growing interest in the company's success strategy. Between 2005 and 2008 alone, Hilton Corp.'s rank in Top-300 Hotel Corporations rating soared from 11th to 3rd, reflecting the growing importance of this hotel chain as one of the world's leading hospitality operators (Cheng, Wang, & Chu 2011, p.214). In 2008, at the time of Hilton's acquisition by the Blackstone Group, the company had a combined workforce of more than 100,000 workers and employees who were employed in 78 nations worldwide (Applegate, Piccoli, & Dev 2008, p.2). Together with the data presented in Table 1, this would enable the reader to conceive of the scope of Hilton Corp.'s global operations.

As of 2000, the Hilton Corp.'s main strategy with respect to the company's growth would emphasize the utilization of aggressive franchising and branding management as the main form of company's expansion. For instance, in 2005, the final return of Hilton International to Hilton Company's fold was negotiated (Applegate, Piccoli, & Dev 2008, p.2). At the same time, the Hilton management embarked on the protracted organic growth strategy and development, so as to guarantee the company's stable growth.

Furthermore, the branding management has always historically been the Hilton's business strategy's crucial component. The company makes use of the number of various brands, including such prominent ones as Hilton Hotels & Resorts, Conrad International, or Embassy Suites. The main focus of all these brands seems to be on the customer's needs, as the company has repeatedly emphasized that the customer well-being is its primary concern. Such programs as the Customers Really Matter (CRM), introduced by Hilton's IT team in 2002, have been used by the company to trace the effects of their customer loyalty programs on Hilton's performance, as well as to recognize the barriers toward the perfect rendering of the company's hospitality services that still need to be breached (Applegate, Piccoli, & Dev 2008, p.4). All of these factors are to be evaluated within the integrative analysis based on the BPM instruments.

A Business Performance Management (BPM) analysis may proceed from the utilization of several indicators for measuring the efficiency of the company's business performance. Venkatraman & Ramanujam (1986) present a three-tier classification of the BPM models commonly encountered in the strategic management literature. In their classification, the BPM analytical models may encompass the financial performance-based models (i.e. the ones that take such indicators as "sales growth, profitability…earnings per share", etc. as the main determinants of the company's business success); the operational performance-focused research approaches that take nonfinancial indicators into account (e.g. "market share, product quality'); and the organizational effectiveness approach, championed by the authors themselves, which would take both data categories into account (Venkatraman & Ramanujam, 1986, pp.803-804). Given the focus of this study and the limitations of this paper, the financial performance approach would be utilized to evaluate Hilton's business performance in the decade of its globalization-driven network growth.

The data from the 2003 to 2006 Hilton Corp. business reports attest to the significant correlation between the brand specifications in question and the financial revenues received by the company. Thus, it is necessary to reproduce them here in the form of Table 2, so as to present a concise picture of the correlation between brand and financial indicators.

Brand	2003	2004	2005	2006
Waldorf-Astoria Collection				
Room				
Revenue	$261,159,914	$289,401,766	$327,954,076	$351,124,552
ADR	$254	$280	$330	$321
RevPAR	$192	$212	$240	$258
RevPAR				
Index	115.2	110.9	111.8	111.4
Conrad International				
Room				
Revenue	$13,922,405	$16,488,158	$24,366,171	$34,027,356
ADR	n/a	$171	$183	$224
RevPAR	$123	$110	$128	$129
RevPAR		94.0		
Index	106.9		90.5	87.6
Hilton Hotels				
Room			$3,030,171,471	$3,334,146,538
Revenue	$2,471,302,966	$2,471,302,966	$138	$149
ADR	$125	$128	$97	$105
RevPAR	$82	$88		
RevPAR			104.7	104.8
Index	105.4	104.8		

Source: Applegate, Piccoli, & Dev 2008.

The following variables should be taken into account while evaluating this result:

- ADR, or Average Daily Rate, measures the mean room rate paid by the hotel guests for the given year;

- RevPAR, or Revenue per Available Room, indicates the revenue produced by the hotel institution per annum on the basis of the number of rooms available for sale for the same period.

- RevPAR Index is a computable comparison index measured via the contrast between the individual brand's index and that of its competitors. As the spatial constraints of this paper would not allow for the more comprehensive elaboration of all Hilton's brands' RevPARs, the limited purposeful sample for the whole dataset was included.

Given the data presented above, it may be surmised that the financial performance of the brand in question is directly correlated with its popularity among the customers. As the data for Hilton Hotels brand demonstrate, its superior financial performance far outstrips that of the other two brands. Hence, it may be concluded that the efficient brand advancement campaigns that have been promoted by the Hilton management for the duration of the 1990s to 2000s enabled the Hilton Hotels brand to acquire the globally significant character. Using the concept of global brands explored by Van Gelder (2005), one may observe that the hotel chain MNCs may have benefitted from their increased brand appeal to the customers.

Further, the issues of unequal competition may be mentioned here. The capacity of the First World-based MNCs to master international hospitality markets has been greatly facilitated by their nations' competitive advantage in the field of technologies and communications. Thus, the formation of globally relevant brand image was probably made easier to these MNCs due to the impact of globally consumed Western hospitality models.

International Hospitality Industry and Labour Market

The problem of labour market transformations in international hospitality industry became a focus for concern in the 1990s, as it became evident that the industry's demand for the high-quality hospitality services delivery may have been blocked by the lack of highly educated workforce in many of the developing nations serving as the Western tourists' favoured destinations (Baum, Amoah, & Spivack 1997, p.222). On the other hand, the growth in casual and part-time employment, as well as the high turnover rates in the national labour markets of both developed and developing nations that became the major recipients of revenues from international tourism, have become one of the problems to be addressed in the course of the strategic management of international hospitality industry (Wood 1997). Together with the problem of de-skilling, this has led to some scholars questioning of the beneficial role of economic globalization with respect to the situation of international hospitality workforce (Baum 1995).

However, the results of the other study point at the other side of the question. As noted by Choi, Woods, & Murrmann (2000), the development of advanced technologies (see next section) and the growing demand for the highly proficient and diversified labour force that is often not met by the adequate labour force supply. This may lead to better working conditions for the knowledge workers deciding to start their careers in the field of tourism and hospitality. At the same time, though, the prevailing employment regimes in modern hospitality services often prioritize labour productivity over fair reward.

As demonstrated by the study of lived experiences of the Polish immigrant workers in British hospitality sector conducted by Janta et al. (2011), the problem of guaranteeing adequate work compensation to the migrant workers is still present at the forefront of the public perception of the international hospitality industry trends. According to the data presented by Janta et al. (2011), as of 2009, more than 109,205 out of 171,940 migrant workers employed in British hospitality and catering sectors were of Polish nationality (Janta et al. 2011, p.1006). As the results of the survey of the sample of these workers' opinion demonstrate, the issues of low work compensation (about £25 per day or lower) and unfair wage cuts are of utmost importance to these workers. Thus, the challenges of accommodating the needs and aspirations of the migrant workers in the First World nations such as the UK should still be addressed if the smooth development of a globalized hospitality industry may proceed.

However, at the same time, one should note that the Third World nations' labour markets have clearly benefited from the growing demand for hospitality services located in these nations. In particular, Egypt and Thailand may be singled out as the beneficiaries of the hospitality services globalization. According to Aish & Badawy (2010), in the period between 2000 and 2006 alone, the overall employment rate in hospitality industry increased by 73%, with the number of tourist villages and similar destinations growing from 503 in 1997 to 1332 in 2006 (2010, p. 3). Similarly, the Thai hospitality industry employment experienced significant growth between 1993 and 2002, with the numbers of workers employed rising from 1.26 million in 1993 to 2.06 million in 2002 (Mephokee 2003, p.5). This rise may have been even more significant but for the late 1990s Asian economic crisis. However, in general, this and similar statistics from other developing nations clearly point at the highly beneficial role of the globalizing hospitality industry in creating new job opportunities for the rapidly growing Third World populations. Given the present circumstances, this may be deemed a positive side to the current economic globalization.

International Hospitality Industry and Globalization of Information Technologies

As it has already been mentioned in the discussion of Hilton Corp.'s customer outreach methods, the utilization of computer-based techniques plays an important role in both the MNCs' and SMEs' strategies for dealing with their customer segments. In particular, the Web services distribution and E-procurement have been playing an increasingly important role for the majority of hospitality operators since at least the late 1990s (O'Connor & Piccoli 2003, p.115). Furthermore, the development of Destination Management Systems (DMS), with their databases encompassing information on the variety of available hotels and other hospitality properties, may be considered one of the important advances of international hospitality industry in this digital epoch.

The growth of Internet as the easily accessible communications medium enabled even the SME operators to participate in the electronic forms of hospitality business by setting their own Web sites, with direct booking options included (O'Connor & Horan 1999). Moreover, the E-procurement instruments enable greater reduction of labour and administrative costs associated with the traditional supplies procurement operations. In particular, this system allowed hospitality operators to establish links with the variety of suppliers worldwide. For instance, according to the data for 2001 alone, the cost savings resulting from the use of E-procurement facilities approximated $3.5 to 4 billion in the USA, and $7 billion globally (O'Connor & Piccoli 2003, p.118). However, the challenges of developing an efficient online Customer Relationship Management (CRM) system still restrict the SMEs' ability to efficiently compete with the hotel chains MNCs, such as Hilton Corp. Hence, the problem of unequal competition still presents itself in this situation.

Globalization and Hospitality Business Strategies

According to Go & Moutinho (2000), the modern sector of international hospitality is challenged by a range of the problems, among which the issues of the branding proliferation and the governmental regulations' discrepancies in various nations take the primary place. Together with the problem of shares' concentration and McDonaldization, this may lead to significant problem for the SMEs that attempt to carve their share of the market in international hospitality industry (Athiyaman and Go 2003, p.146). However, some preliminary recommendations on the development of stable and unique international hospitality may be derived from the examples of successful business strategies of the leading hospitality market players.

The diversification and sustainable development strategies are frequently cited as key to the success of the commercial ventures in modern hospitality industry (Go & Appelman 2001). For instance, the impending McDonaldization of Italian restaurant industry in the 1980s led to the development of a grassroots "Slow Food" movement that managed to at least partially recuperate the ground lost by domestic food companies (Athiyaman and Go 2003, p.146). Similarly, the case study of Hilton Corp. that has been discussed points at the need for greater brand diversification that might enable the company to appeal to different customer segments, while staying faithful to its core constituency. In general, though, the competitive life cycles of the hospitality products are necessarily limited. Therefore, the development of new and competitive brands is a must to every company that plans to remain in the market for the significant amount of time.

Conclusion

Having reviewed the research data in question, one may now turn to the development of generalized conclusions on the research subject. First, the globalization of the hospitality services is greatly facilitated by the spread of Western hospitality brands that may then provide the hotel chains MNCs with better access options to the varied national markets. At the same time, judging from the example of Hilton Hotel Corp., the commercial success and eventual monopolization of international hotel services by the handful of Western-based multinationals might lead to the development of better and more universal customer relationship standards that would in turn benefit the hospitality sector at large.

Second, in spite of the problem of precarious employment, the international hospitality sector has been providing larger numbers of workers with job opportunities since 1990s than ever before. In particular, such nations as Thailand and Egypt have secured substantial revenues from the modern hospitality industry. Hence, the labour market impact of globalization in hospitality may be deemed generally beneficial, while some important problems still present themselves to the public.

Third, the IT revolution brought about by the respective development in the 1990s and 2000s has both made international hospitality industry more dependent on digital media and environments (for advertising its products, etc.) and enabled greater number of customers worldwide to partake in the opportunities offered by the globalizing world. Therefore, the globalization of information and communications services opened new venues for the development of a more integrated hospitality sector.

Finally, the business strategies of major companies and SMEs oriented towards hospitality sector are increasingly based on the global branding option. The growth of globalizing trends in mass communications and tourism directly sustain these companies' business, for without the opportunities offered by globalization, it would be actually untenable. Thus, further economic and cultural globalization may bring greater opportunities to both businesses and customers, enhancing general performance of international hospitality industry.

Reference List

Aish, E A, & Badawy, N A A A 2010, 'The factors influencing customers' complaining intentions within the hospitality industry in Egypt,' accessed on 17 December 2012, <http://icbme.yasar.edu.tr/e-proceedings/Full%20Papers/Nesma%20Ammar.pdf>

Applegate, L M, Piccoli, G, & Dev, C 2008, 'Hilton hotels: brand differentiation through customer relationship management,' accessed on 18 December 2012, <http://202.120.148.199/Files/Hilton+Hotels.pdf>

Athiyaman, A, & Go, F 2003, 'Strategic choices in the international hospitality industry,' in B Brotherton (ed.), *The international hospitality industry: structure, characteristics and issues,* Butterworth-Heinemann, Oxford, pp.142-160.

Baum, T 1995, *Managing human resources in the European tourism and hospitality industry: a strategic approach,* Chapman & Hall, London.

Baum, T, Amoah, V, & Spivack, S 1997, 'Policy dimensions of human resource management in the tourism and hospitality industry,' *International Journal of Contemporary Hospitality Management,* Vol. 9, No.5-6, pp.221-229.

Cheng, Y-C, Wang, W-C, & Chu, Y-C 2011, 'A case study on the business performance management of Hilton Hotels Corporation,' *International Journal of Business and Management,* Vol. 4, No. 2, pp.213-218.

Choi, J-G, Woods, R H, & Murrmann, S K 2000, 'International labor markets and the migration of labor forces as an alternative solution for labor shortages in the hospitality industry,' *International Journal of Contemporary Hospitality Management,* Vol. 12, No.1, pp.61-67.

Das, V, & De Groote, P 2008, 'Globalisation in hotel chains. Case study: profile of the Belgian business traveller,' accessed on 18 December 2012, <http://doclib.uhasselt.be/dspace/bitstream/1942/10622/2/HotechainsLiegefinal.pdf>

Hall, S 1992, 'The question of cultural identity,' in S Hall, D Held & T McCrew (eds.), *Modernity and its futures,* Polity Press, Oxford, pp.274-316.

Go, F, & Appelman, 2001, 'Achieving global competitiveness in SMEs by building trust in inter-firm alliances,' in S Wahab & C Cooper (eds.), *Tourism in the age of globalisation,* Routledge, London, pp.183-197.

Go, F, & Moutinho, L 2000, 'International tourist management,' in L. Moutinho (ed.), *Strategic management in tourism,* CABI, Oxford, pp.315-355.

Janta, H, Ladkin, A, Brown, L, & Lugosi, P 2011, 'Employment experiences of Polish migrant workers in the UK hospitality sector,' *Tourism Management,* Vol. 32, No.5, pp.1006-1019.

Knowles, T, Diamantis, D, & El Mourhabi, J 2004, *The globalization of tourism and hospitality: a strategic perspective,* Thomson, London.

Mephokee, C 2003, 'Thai labour market in transition toward a knowledge-based economy,' in M Makishima & S Suksiriserkul (eds.), *Human resource development toward a knowledge-based economy: the case of Thailand,* Institute of Developing Economies, Japan External Trade Organization, Chuba, Japan.

O'Connor, P, & Horan, P 1999, 'An analysis of web reservation facilities in the top 50 international hotel chains,' *International Journal of Hospitality Information Technology,* Vol.1, No.1, pp.77-87.

O'Connor, P, & Piccoli, G 2003, 'The impact of information technology,' in B Brotherton (ed.), *The international hospitality industry: structure, characteristics and issues,* Butterworth-Heinemann, Oxford, pp.110-125.

Van Gelder, S 2005, *Global brand strategy: unlocking branding potential across countries, cultures, and markets,* 2nd edn, Kogan Page Limited, London.

Venkatraman, N, & Ramanujam, V 1986, 'Measurement of business performance in strategy research: a comparison of approaches,' *The Academy of Management Review,* Vol. 11, No. 4, pp.801-814.

Wood, R C 1997, *Working in hotel and catering,* 2nd edn, International Thomson Business Press, London.